ASK ANYTHING

INTERVIEW SUCCESSFULLY AND GET THE JOB YOU WANT

PHILIP HESS, MBA

Published by Tremendous Leadership

PO Box 267 • Boiling Springs, PA 17007

(800) 233 - 2665 • *www.TremendousLeadership.com*

Tremendous Leadership's titles may be bulk purchased for business or promotional use or for special sales. Please contact Tremendous Leadership for more information.

ISBN-13 978-1-949033-62-5

Designed and Made in the United States of America

Contents

Dedication

To my wife Janet, the love of my life, and for all her support for over 55 years. To my children John, Stephen, Susan, and their families for always putting up with my wild ideas and many corporate relocations.

Before You Begin

The person sitting across from you has limited knowledge of your identity and capabilities. Yet, here you are, about to engage in a crucial interaction that could change the trajectory of your entire life. And since you never get a second chance to make a first impression, the best version of you must show up for this and every interview.

Phil Hess shows you how to achieve this lofty goal every time you sit across from a prospective employer, promoter, or selection committee. Phil has six decades of experience in watching, critiquing, and coaching the interview process. He knows precisely what will seal the deal and what causes employers to non-select.

In this brief read, you'll find a toolbox filled with actionable steps so you can prepare, practice, and perform the perfect showcase of your personality and talents. Ninety percent of success in any endeavor is in the preparation, and interviewing is no exception. So, take some time to read this gem, and do what it tells you to do. Then watch the results hit your inbox or mailbox.

No matter what professional stage you

find yourself in, these strategies are tried and true. There's no secret to getting hired; there is only science. And Phil's tremendous track record of helping others get that job speaks to his expertise. So put his years of knowledge and experience to work in your job search. You'll be able to confidently state, "Ask Me Anything!"

And congratulations in advance for knocking their socks off during the interview and getting that offer. Well done!

Dr. Tracey C. Jones
President, Tremendous Leadership

"Tell Me About Yourself"

Whether interviewing for a new job, seeking acceptance into an educational program, or vying for a promotion, hearing these four words can strike fear and a virtual fight or flight response in many people. This book enables you to confidently answer that question and the ones to follow.

I remember my first interview for a management trainee position. I wanted the job so badly, and I was so nervous I almost felt like I would jump out of my skin. I knew the directions to the interview site. I had a pressed suit and shirt, and I thought I was prepared. But, as it turned out, I was not in the least prepared for what was about to take place.

I had read in interview books to make sure to maintain good eye contact. I remember staring intently at one of my interviewer's eyes. I stared to the point that my ears started to ring, and I started experiencing tunnel vision.

"Oh, my goodness, I'm hypnotizing myself! I think I might pass out!" My thoughts raced desperately. "How do I look away from his eye? What do I do now?" Certainly, this was not the time or place to start practicing my interview skills.

Somehow, I made it through that interview without hitting the floor in a comatose state. Filled with relief after it was over, I asked for the office of the person who had arranged the interview for me. Two large mahogany doors later, I found myself in the presence of two company vice presidents, one of whom had served as United States Assistant Secretary of State during the Kennedy and Johnson presidencies. Despite my shock, I felt less nervous in this setting than in my formal interview and was able to carry on a casual but meaningful conversation with the top two executives in the eastern region of Sears. Sears was the largest retailer in the world at that time, the company with whom I very much wanted a job.

To my delight, I received a job offer. Had my initiative in requesting an interview made a good first impression? Had my personal walk down the hall to the executive suite to offer my gratitude for the interview made a significant impact? Did those follow-up "Thank You" letters make a difference? I will never know. I just had to rest in the satisfaction of a job offer and continue to do my best in future interviews with government, retail, manufacturing, and insurance companies.

Would you believe I received offers after each of these interviews? I wondered if that was because I had learned from my first experience or because I felt more relaxed with an offer in my pocket. Again, I will never know, just as most candidates will not know why they were offered a specific job.

Despite the other job offers, I eventually accepted the very first one, and started my dream job with Sears. My 38-year career led me to 9 different cities and 15 different management assignments. One of my assignments over the years, in combination with my normal unit management responsibilities, was as a college recruiter. The company provided me extensive training from human resources experts and psychologists in how to conduct interviews and evaluate candidates. I traveled to campuses for first interviews and then to corporate offices for "second looks." These "second looks" included testing, several forms of interviews, and round table discussion observations in which we presented candidates with problems and observed as the candidates worked together to solve the problems through their group interactions.

Throughout my career, I have always taken an interest in helping people; particularly in helping the right person find the right job. The wealth of information I received in training and the subsequent experiences interviewing thousands of candidates allowed me to develop an interview preparation technique that encourages applicants to look at the interview process as a strategic plan.

Process

A good process produces good results.
—Nick Saban

Developed over 50 years, this process has several dynamic phases. If you commit to following the system, it will guide you to identify your values and create a plan that will help you meet your goals. Armed with a personalized strategy enabling you to confidently answer virtually any question with a short one-to-two-minute response, you will find yourself more relaxed even for your first interview. From how to discover your strengths and how to have good eye contact, to how to open strong and how to ask for the job, this process covers all the bases. All that will be left is for you to practice.

My system has been applied to all types of job markets including ed-

ucation, finance, banking, administration, accounting, and law enforcement, just to name a few. It works for live interviews as well as phone and virtual interviews. It has proven successful for new hires, for students interviewing for a school or scholarship, and for experienced employees seeking a wage increase or promotion. In fact, my system has worked for every candidate who has taken the time to practice their preparation skills and develop a great strategy! This amazing success is why I decided to write my unique process down in this book to help others obtain the jobs, education, and promotions they deserve.

Haste Makes Waste

If you go slow, you go fast.

I always try to incorporate this old saying into my planning. I can pick up a newspaper or open job postings online and think that I have found the perfect job for me, but if I have not properly prepared for my job search, the chances of wasting my time are great. While it may start with writing a resume (a little more on that later) and perusing job postings, a successful job search is not that simple.

When I look at 100 candidates, probably 75 percent will work hard crafting and proofing a resume with all the latest buzz words and phrases. Out of the same 100 candidates, only 2 percent will go the extra mile in preparing for an interview. If you are willing to put in the extra work, you can find yourself in this 2 percent, and you won't have to worry about 98 other applicants who are not properly prepared for their interviews.

The reality is that the interview process is a "carryover process." What does that mean? Even though it may not be a common occurrence, most of us will face official interviews at least several times in our lives. Beyond that, each of us is constantly being informally evaluated throughout life for assignments, invitations, relationships, and more. Therefore, the interview process is one that we need to develop and practice because it will carryover repeatedly throughout our lives.

My latest college client was quite nervous about her job search. But, because of her preparation, she had a successful first interview and was even more comfortable in her second and third interviews. With more than one offer, she broke into a state-of-the-art industry as a new graduate.

While it won't be easy, if properly executed, this process will give you the confidence to walk into an interview saying, "Ask me anything." And it will fill you with pride as you walk out saying, "I did my best."

If you aren't willing to take the time to create a strategy, you may obtain a job, but do you think you will be as successful as the person who is willing to prepare? The answer is, no.

The secret of every man who has ever been successful lies in the fact that he formed the habit of doing things that failures don't like to do.
—Albert E. N. Gray

For those whom I am coaching or advising in developing a motivated mindset, I encourage them to read a little essay entitled "The Common Denominator of Success." In 1940, Albert Gray, an official of Prudential Insurance Company of America, spoke at the National Association of Life Underwriters at their annual convention in Philadelphia. In just under 3,000 words, Gray describes his belief that successful people develop the habits of doing what unsuccessful people do not want to do. And they do it with purpose.

A simple online search will bring up free versions of "The Common Denominator of Success" in print and audio. You can also pick up copies for your friends and team members at my publisher's site, *www.TremendousLeadership.com*. Take a few minutes right now to read or listen to it. I promise, it will change your life forever.

Preparation

Shorten the path to success by lengthening the hours of preparation.

—Captain Dalton E. Brady

Now that you know why you should take the time to develop an interview strategy, you should approach this process like a business. That's one reason you will see me use business terminology throughout this book, words like strategy, vision, and mission. Getting a job is a job, and it requires daily work. You must prepare, and you must practice. Make a schedule, and commit to sticking to it as you work your way through the phases of this process: formulation, internal audit, external audit, implementation, and review.

Strategy Formulation: Vision and Mission

A strategy is a plan that will allow you to achieve a goal, and the first step in developing any strategy is a thorough analysis. Start by asking yourself, **"What is my ideal job?"** Think about what you want to do, imagine where you want to go, and work from there.

During this phase, you will develop your personal vision statement and a mission statement. **Your vision statement will describe what you want to become or accomplish, while your mission statement will describe the ideals that will aid you in attaining your vision.** Some say a vision is a goal statement, and a mission is a value statement. I like to think of your mission statement as a compass setting for the direction you will move toward your vision statement. Your values keep you on course to reach your goal.

Here is a simplified example. Let's say your vision statement is "Find a job." When you are working towards your goal of finding a job, then your mission statement might include values such as being a good communicator, being efficient and productive, and being a problem solver.

It is important to take the time to identify goals and values you can cherish, and it will take time. Taking your time in developing your vision and mission statements may mean you could spend a week or more giving it thorough consideration. **Do not rush this phase. Every value in your mission should support the attainment of your vision.** Every decision you make must support your goal. If you decide to go a different direction and not follow your mission, then you run the risk of not obtaining your goal. For example, if part of your mission is to be a good communicator, as suggested above, in order to reach your vision of a choice job, then you must practice for your interview. If you do not practice, you are ignoring your mission, and you may not reach your goal.

You also have to know that you may need to come back and adjust your vision and mission statements as you work your way through this process. For example, your values should reflect a good combination of both your strengths and potential job descriptions, as you will discover in the next phases.

The Internal Audit: Look Inside Yourself

Perhaps you've heard the term **SWOT analysis** used in the business world. Just as companies use this tool in planning, an internal audit helps you identify your strengths (**S**), weaknesses (**W**), opportunities (**O**), and threats (**T**).

Have you had people tell you that you are a good communicator or that you are a hard worker? These are examples of internal strengths that you should be proud of and can rely on to overcome weakness or to grasp hold of opportunities.

While strengths and weaknesses describe personal characteristics, an opportunity or threat refers to independent elements that may affect you. For example, you may not have a reliable car to get you to work on time each day. That could be a threat that needs to be remedied in order for you to get your dream job. Begin your internal audit by considering the following questions and be thorough and honest in your answers:

Strengths

1. What training or education have you completed?

2. Where do you excel? What are your best skills?
3. What would be your ideal occupation?
4. How do you like to spend your time?
5. What causes people to like you or come to you for help?
6. Where do you make the biggest contribution?

Weaknesses

1. What type of situations or events worry you?
2. What is your worst subject?
3. What holds you back from what you want to do?

Opportunities

1. How much time can you spend on your job?
2. Are you able to relocate?
3. What are your plans for further education?

Threats

1. Can you work unsupervised?
2. Do you have time or travel restrictions?
3. Do you have other obligations that interfere with your time?

These are just some of the questions that can help you to identify what factors make you an outstanding candidate compared to your competition.

It is important to note that your internal audit will need to be updated as factors in your life change. Perhaps you took a class in accounting and have learned new skills. Or maybe you participated in a marketing research study, and it sparked a new interest.

The internal audit process will also help with writing your resume. Although this is not a book about how to write a resume, I will say that you always need to keep your resume up to date. You never know when someone may want to talk to you about an opportunity, so you need to stay prepared. If you have a good strategy, you can then, and only then, jump on that opportunity. Unless you are properly prepared, you will find the experience frustrating. I have helped people who were up for civil service promotions and had to submit a resume. It was a huge undertaking to reconstruct a 30-year career to be eligible for a promotion. I am of retirement age now, but I still keep several current resumes: one for accounting, one for teaching, and one for preaching.

In addition, you must remember that candidates will always be reviewed against a job description. While companies know that few, if any, candidates will meet 100 percent of the job qualifications, there are several common factors that almost all companies are looking for in candidates. Part of leveraging your strengths is understanding how they line up with job descriptions. This strategy is not intended to mold your experiences to fit a job description. Instead, it is geared to have you realize that your experiences have prepared you for a job.

Are You a Good Candidate?

There are few jobs that do not require basic digital literacy. Be straightforward in the description of your skill level and provide a plan for how you intend to improve any shortcomings.

Many institutions today are also stressing that employees must show adaptability to change. People say the only thing constant is change. How do you handle the pressure of change? Evaluate the ways in which you have adjusted to remote learning or work, and highlight examples of your resilience that show you are prepared to make necessary changes as a future employee of the company.

I know someone who was feeling added pressure at work due to COVID-19 social distancing protocols; but by scheduling daily check-ins with friends via video calls those relationships grew more robust, and a new communication system emerged. This is a good example of how creativity can turn a seemingly negative change into a positive.

A good candidate will always have to be a problem solver, so you should review your strengths for how you have solved problems in the past. Turn a negative into a positive by talking about a problem you've faced and how you reacted to it.

If someone buys a product that features stainless steel construction, they have been sold on the benefits of an item that is long-lasting and easy to clean. Features sell. Benefits are what we buy.

Employment decisions are no different. Employers have problems they need to solve, and they want to know how successful you will be at solving them. They need to be sold on the benefits they will receive from your employment. Will you make their jobs easier and more profitable? The strengths you discover in the internal audit will solve the company problems you will determine in the external audit. You must prove that you possess the features to solve problems in effective ways by giving examples of what you have previously accomplished. Examples make the sale.

Lead By Example

A client once told me about jumping into an elevator at his home office some ten years after his initial job interview, and the person who interviewed him was in the elevator, recognized him, and said, "Hi Steve, how are you? You know, I still remember how you solved your summer job problem by creating a window cleaning business. I tell my kids that story all the time." Steve's story doesn't surprise me at all because I can still remember good examples given to me by candidates even 40 years after the interviews.

It is not enough to know and share your personal strengths, weaknesses, opportunities, and threats. You must develop stories, specific examples of what you have accomplished, that will add credibility to your answers and demonstrate how your strengths and values can benefit a company.

Don't say, "I am a team player," without adding, "For example there was a time when...."

When someone says, "I'm energetic" or

"I'm a team player," I think to myself, "So what? Everyone says that." I call these "Scout Law interviews." The Scout Law says that a Scout is "trustworthy, loyal, helpful, friendly, courteous, kind, obedient, cheerful, thrifty, brave, clean, and reverent." Anyone can claim to have these qualities, but it is the real-life examples that back up the statements that are most important.

Always support any answer with an example whenever possible, and practice running through your examples along with your answers.

People will remember impactful examples long after more routine answers from numerous interviews begin to blur together. Those examples of how you can meet a company's needs as a problem solver or communicator are what you want them to remember about you when they get ready to make their decisions.

During the interview process, each interview is compared to the others, and the best file is always put on the top. You want to stay on the top, and your specific examples make the difference between just answers and memorable, seal-the-deal statements.

External Audit

Look Beyond Yourself

Every interview candidate should do this exercise, but few people do. In addition to looking inside yourself, you also must look at the outside world and determine the strengths, weaknesses, opportunities, and threats for external factors. For example, if working remotely is an option, you might consider this an opportunity. Or if the unemployment level is high, competition for jobs will be greater. This could be a threat to your job search.

When you perform an external audit, you want to examine your selected industry and potential employers. You might consider a visit to one of their locations or facilities. I have walked around campuses, through libraries, and into campus bookstores before interviews for adjunct professor positions. I have sat in parking lots to observe the dress of associates going into the location. I have walked in the lobbies of organizations and talked to the receptionists, asking for their latest brochures or where I would find the Human Resources office.

If you are not close to the location, then

company or organizational websites, chat sites, and news articles can provide valuable information, such as when a company was founded or by whom. You can look around the area virtually to see parking, hotels, apartments, parks, etc. You can look at the crime statistics for the area.

Make sure you do your audit before an interview so you can be confident that if given the opportunity you would want to accept the offer. Being aware of these external factors not only improves your confidence in an interview, it can also allow you to make knowledgeable comments about the company. Anything that makes you a more well-informed candidate is of vital importance.

Here is a list of possible questions for an external audit of a recruiting organization:

Strengths

1. Does the company or organization have a favorable reputation?
2. Is the company or organization in a healthy financial state?
3. What advantages does this company or organization have over competitors?

Weaknesses

1. Is the company or organization located in an unsafe or inconvenient area

or somewhere you would be unwilling to move?
2. What disadvantages does this company or organization have compared to others?
3. Do employees speak negatively of the work environment on chat forums?

Opportunities

1. What is the company's strategy for the future?
2. Are there plans for expansion or right-sizing?
3. Is competition pushing them to seek innovation?

Threats

1. What problems do they want you to handle?
2. Is there a high turnover of employees?
3. Does the company have balance sheet problems?

Implementation

Where the Rubber Meets the Road

In recruiting and hiring interviews, I can tell immediately if people have prepared. Like other interviewers, I often recognize when candidates give answers with little substance or just say whatever they think we want to hear. But, with your properly prepared strategy that aligns with your goals and values, you will have the satisfaction of not spitting out canned responses.

It would be impossible to provide an exhaustive list of interview questions here. (You can easily search "common interview questions" online.) We will, however, discuss ten questions that, when examined and practiced in light of your personal strategy, will prepare you for just about any question an interviewer may throw your way.

1. Tell me about yourself?
2. Why are you interested in this position?
3. How do you learn best?
4. What is your biggest weakness?
5. What is your greatest strength?
6. What are you most proud of?
7. If you could change anything over the last five years, what would it be?
8. Where do you see yourself in five years?
9. Do you have any questions for me?
10. Is there anything you want to add?

Obviously, these are not the only questions you will be asked in interviews. For example, I prefer to ask more probing questions like, "Can you give me an example of a time when you went above and beyond what was expected to help a group, a fellow classmate, a customer, or a stranger?" I often hear hems and haws when I ask that question. Sometimes, candidates will stall for time by saying, "That is a good question," or "Can you repeat that question?"

But if you have practiced well-developed answers with examples to these ten questions, you can imagine how you can easily adapt your responses to one of these questions (such as "What's your biggest strength?" or "What are you most proud of?") to answer my more in-depth question.

Finding the Best Answer

Let's take a look at one of the other questions on this list: How do you learn? This is a question that *Harvard Business Review* suggests every interviewer ask because it gives them insight into a candidate's trainability. All of us respond differently to written, spoken, and visual instructions, and today it is more important than ever to see how a future employee learns and communicates. To develop your answer and an applicable example to such a question, think about something you have learned lately? For example, how have you adapted to remote learning? Or what did you learn from your recent internship?

One person told me of an interviewer who asked, "If I told you I wanted you to walk backwards while at work, what salary would you want?"

"Twice what you would pay me to walk forward at work."

The candidate received an offer, so the manager must have appreciated the quick response. I might have said, "Since it is twice as hard to walk backward, I would expect a premium pay. At 40 hours a week, an associate works 2,080 hours a year, so at $20 per hour that would be $40,160 a year; so, I would expect $40 per hour or $80,320 a year." An answer like that shows that you can think fast, you know how to evaluate a salary offer, and you value the complexity of the job.

Sometimes interviewers just want to see how logically a candidate will approach a question. One graduate school candidate was asked, "Could you give me an estimate of how many golf balls are in the air right now?" The candidate proceeded to calculate aloud, "Well, we have to consider the weather, the time of day in different parts of the world..." and went on to give the logic for the answer. Another candidate was asked, "Can you tell me how many dairy cows are in the US?" The person explained how they would calculate an estimate with information obtained through online research of the dairy industry.

I don't share these examples to make you more nervous, but that you will feel prepared for the unusual. If a question like this or a question you haven't thought of comes up in your interview, stay focused but flexible and remember to pull from answers and examples you have practiced. Explain your reasoning as you answer difficult or unexpected questions because how you react to the unexpected and solve problems is what interviewers are looking for. **Be careful not to make sarcastic or smug comments that might embarrass the interviewer.**

You should also be aware that there are questions that should never be asked in an interview, questions about marital status, transportation, and religion are some. You can search online for questions you do not have to answer. If asked, you can decline to answer these questions by saying something like, "I am aware that could be an issue of concern for some individuals, but I am able to perform the duties of this position as assigned, and that matter will not interfere with my performance."

Many interview books say that you should prepare by writing down your answers. Now, I believe strongly in developing answers to these questions with specific examples to support them. But, let me ask you a question: Are you going to be able to use notes in most interviews? Are you going to have a teleprompter? The obvious answer is no. **I suggest you read each of the above questions aloud and talk through your responses to develop your best one-to-two-minute answers.** Try different responses. Record your answers, and play them back to yourself. With recordings you will more easily notice your most used word phrases. Do you like your tone, your energy level? Does your answer make sense? Is it how you want an interviewer to remember your response?

As you continue the process of talking

out loud, hearing yourself speak, and listening to your recordings, your answers should become more natural and conversational, smoother and more coherent. You will begin to develop a more articulate delivery with an appropriate use of pauses and inflections in your voice. Your flow of words during interviews will reflect what you have practiced and heard in your recordings. This process will not only make your answers sound more professional, but your preparations will enable you to be more relaxed during interviews.

I had a client recently who, after 30 years with her current company, was in search of more opportunities. After a year of trying on her own, she came to me for coaching. She used this method, and after she heard how she answered the questions and adjusted her responses accordingly, she obtained an offer on her first interview because she had become more effectively able to relay her skills and talents in an efficient manner.

Start Strong

Many say that an interviewer will decide within the first two minutes whether or not an applicant is a good fit for their organization. "Tell me about yourself," which is more often than not the opening question, is an opportunity for you to establish the tone of your interview, grabbing the interviewer's interest immediately. You may feel nervous, but you can't afford to sound timid or unsure.

An interviewer's time is valuable, and if you have spent the time practicing how you will answer this question, your confidence will show that you are not one to waste time. The more productive you can be, the more engaged your interviewer will be. A well-developed communication style lets them know that you are a good candidate, and companies jump on candidates who are strong communicators.

Silence is Golden

One of the tactics an interviewer may use is to be silent. Most people tend not to like silence, especially in an interview. While it can feel like there is nothing more deadly to a conversation than silence, a silent pause may actually stimulate conversation. Sometimes a half-smile or a slightly wider-eyed look from an interviewer can probe for more information, prompting a candidate to start talking. That can be good or bad. **I advise my clients that if this happens to relax and say, "Would you like to hear more about that?" This guards against rambling or repeating answers you have already given and will show confidence.**

If you do not hear or understand a question, politely ask your interviewer to repeat the question or ask for clarification. If there is a language or accent barrier to clear communication, always be sure you have heard the interviewer correctly before you respond.

The Million Dollar Question

Even though I didn't include it in my list of ten, you should be prepared with a response should the salary question arise. Let's just admit it, we all have a salary in mind. Each career path has a salary range, so look at the latest trends on the Internet and start there. You may want to begin your response with something like, "I know there is a basic salary range for this position, but it also depends on the benefit package. Could you tell me what benefits would be considered part of my compensation?" If they want you to offer a salary, then they should be willing to give you the parameters because bonuses, overtime, and compensation time bring up valid questions.

You should also know that 2,080 hours is a normal work year for a full-time employee. If they say they can start you at $25 an hour, know that it is in the $50,000 range, specifically $52,000. If they say, "We can offer you $65,000, plus bonus," then you know it is in the $30 per hour range, specifically $31.25 an hour. Doing some of these calculations ahead of time and knowing some basic figures can help you think on your feet in an interview. Many people will say, "I know the average is approximately $65,000 a year. But with my experience, I would like to discuss the possibilities of more." If asked to write a salary amount on an application, the best way is to write "open" or "$65,000 + or -" or "$65,000 range."

Try to be specific, but remember anything is negotiable. The sooner you get into the right job, the more successful you will become. But also know that the first individual to give something up is often the one to lose the most.

To put all of this into perspective, the average business major's beginning salary of $57,765 in 2021 will compound to career earnings of over $5,300,000. If you are negotiating a $5,000,000 career, it is important for you to start with the pay you deserve.

The Perfect Ending

Along with the first question, the final question in an interview is of utmost importance. Spend extra time working on these two. Also, like the first question, the last question in an interview is almost always the same. Your final answer can be the point of demarcation between just an interview and a job offer. That is the moment of truth when you can reinforce your desire to be remembered as their top candidate. You have shown your best communication skills, giving memorable examples and asking pertinent questions. Your interviewer asks, "Is there anything else you would like to add or discuss?"

Don't ask what one of my clients did: "So when do I start?"

But, if you are sincerely interested and would take a job offer, then you must ask for the job. If you are not willing to ask for the job, they are most likely not interested in hiring you. That is a harsh statement, but it's true.

To ask for a job, say something like this:

"Thank you for this interview, I hope that through my resume and our discussion you have seen that I am well prepared to fill your needs for this position. I hope that my preparation and experiences make me an outstanding candidate. After talking to you, I am sure that I can make a difference in your organization, and I would like to have the opportunity to make that difference."

Practice

If you don't practice, you don't deserve to win.

—Andre Agassi

You have no doubt heard, "Practice makes perfect." Maybe you've even heard, "Practice makes permanent." One thing I can say, for sure, "Practice makes prepared." And that is the difference between this process and other interview preparation programs. Practice will give you the confidence to say, "Ask me anything."

Hit Record

You do not have to write out answers, but you

do have to record them. You should use either audio or audio/video, and you must play the recordings back to yourself. If you are not willing to do this exercise, you will not be ready for your best interview.

This is another big advantage in this strategy over others. I stress the need to hear yourself, the words you use, the tone of your voice. Are you enthusiastic? How fast are you talking? Do you say, "ahh," "you know," or any other filler phrases that show lack of communication skills and practice?

You are probably thinking, "I can work out the answer in my mind, I will know what to say." True, you could do that. But since we think faster than we speak, once we try to put our thoughts into words for the first time, we end up stumbling over the words and adding those fillers.

As I describe in "Find the Best Answer" earlier in the book, go through your questions and record your answers. Do this several times. Practice, practice, but do *not* memorize your answers. Instead, rely on the repetition of practice to allow you to generate natural responses with each question.

A friend's son had a virtual interview, and he was so nervous he made the family leave the house so they could not hear his responses. If he had practiced aloud and heard his answers replayed, he would probably have felt better prepared and more confident, even if his family did overhear him.

Mock It To Me

The next step is to practice an interview. These are often called "mock interviews," and they can be vital in providing feedback on your interview skills and helping you feel prepared to do your best.

A college placement office once asked me to work with a young man because they could not determine why he was not seeing success in his job search. In a practice interview, he described the way he helped a fellow associate whose car wouldn't start by leaving his garage attendant position to drive several blocks to pick up his shift replacement. When I pointed out that he just told me he had abandoned his post, putting his customers' cars and assets at risk, he was shocked. He obviously had not really heard what he was saying and, therefore, was not prepared.

Out of this same discussion, we established that he worked the overnight shift while taking college courses full time. How impressive! I told him to make sure he used that as an example of his exceptional work ethic. He did and received an offer at his next interview.

Consider finding someone, a coach, teacher, parent, or family friend, who will do a practice interview with you and film it. You can film a self-interview if you do not have anyone to assist. Ask or review how you could improve on the key elements of a first interview. This type of practice helps significantly in building your strategy.

Presentation

Always put your best foot forward because you never know where it may lead you.

—Stephan Labossiere

Interview Etiquette

In addition to practicing your answers to possible interview questions, you should also review your interview etiquette, or how you conduct yourself in an interview.

In an actual interview, you should wait to be told where to sit and only sit when the interviewer is starting to sit. Once seated, keep both feet on the floor rather than crossing your legs. You want to seem natural and comfortable, but don't slouch like you're watching TV at home. If that sounds anything but natural, you should probably add this to your interview practice time. These factors are also important for virtual interviews because interviewers can tell if you are slumping even if they can't see your entire body.

The Eyes Have It

Remember how I nearly hypnotized myself during my first interview? I had been told that eye contact was important, but I had no idea how to do this without staring my interviewer down. The best way to have good, effective eye contact is to glance casually from one eye to another and be willing to look away on occasion as you think. If for some reason your interviewers' eyes tend to make you nervous, just stare at the bridge of their nose. They will never know that you are not looking them in the eyes.

And speaking of eyes, did you know that eye movement can be an indication of truthfulness? If you ask me a question, and

I lift my eyes up and to my left, I am probably searching back in my memory for the answer. However, if I raise my eyes up and to my right, there's a greater likelihood that I am making up my answer. This is a good tendency to be aware of and to watch for on any video playback.

Express Yourself

Also pay attention to your mannerisms. Body language can be just as important as eye contact. Once, when my granddaughter interviewed for a new high school, she was so nervous that she played with an aluminum candy wrapper to the point that her fingers became discolored from the ink. It can be a natural tendency to fidget with a pen, ring, or watch, or to grab at your clothes or legs during an interview when you haven't practiced what to do with your hands. Instead try using casual gestures to keep you relaxed and to show good communication skills.

Dress for Success

You want to dress a little more formally for an interview than the described dress code or observed standard. Have your clothes ready in advance, making sure they are clean and well-pressed. Add only minimal jewelry, if any, with no obtrusive lapel or tie pins. Try to avoid perfume or cologne, relying instead on properly trimmed and groomed hair, facial hair, and nails. While you should always eat and be well hydrated before an interview. Be cautious about eating or drinking once you are dressed when that last-minute snack or cup of coffee could stain.

When you are getting your clothes ready for your interview, you should also gather anything you need to take to your interview. **Along with your up-to-date resume, I suggest that you have personal business cards. You can have them made at most business supply stores, sometimes while you wait.** You can also print some with your personal computer using the proper weight paper. Put your contact information on the front and your skills and educational information on the back. If you are paying for both sides of the cards, use both sides.

Also purchase high-quality note cards and envelopes ahead of time. Place your return address and stamps on the envelopes so they are ready to go when you need them right after an interview. (We'll talk more about "Thank You" notes later.) If possible, have a nice business folder to carry extra resumes, gather business cards, or take notes. All of these suggestions will help set you apart from your competition and encourage your interviewer to remember you.

You're Never Fully Dressed Without a Smile

Did you know that it is a proven fact that if you hold a small, half-smile, your body will produce endorphins that tend to relax you? I call it the "Mona Lisa Smile," relaxed, friendly, and yet serious. The next time you are in a situation that has you feeling nervous, apply a "Mona Lisa Smile" and see how it works.

Raise Your Voice

As you have discovered, the tone of your voice can reflect enthusiasm, excitement, and confidence. But it can also sound nervous, sleepy, and bored. You should always warm up your voice before an interview. Run through low- to high-pitch sounds several times so that you feel alert and have a crisp, clear resonance. Vibrating your lips and wagging your tongue may sound funny, but so is your voice if the first words it utters are "Good Morning" in your interview.

On Time is Late

Be on time. There is nothing worse than being stuck in a traffic jam on the way to an interview. For this reason, many suggest it is actually best to be slightly early. I suggest that, beyond being early on the day of your interview, you drive to the interview site the day before if possible. This allows you to consider possible interruptions to your route and to determine where you will park and enter the building. If you go the day before, you may also be able to make a judgment on dress by seeing other employees coming and going. Even with this route rehearsal, plan to arrive before your interview time. If you arrive too early to go inside, you can sit outside or take a walk, and you will still have time to go to the restroom so you can avoid any uncomfortable situations.

Virtual and Phone Interviews

I asked in "Finding the Best Answer" whether

you would be able to use notes during most interviews. Well, a virtual or phone interview is the exception. During these interviews, you can create a list of the most important examples of what you have to offer. You can place the list on the wall right above the camera of the computer or on the desk for a phone interview. I have told candidates to place post-it notes around the outside edges of your computer so you can glance at them and make sure you point out the noted strengths and examples. As you discuss the items, you can check them off or know that you covered them.

In a virtual interview, it is important for you to look at the camera. When giving a response, imagine a person's face at the location of your camera. Some people affix a picture of a face on the top edge of their computer, and they talk to that face. All these tricks will allow you to look natural and relaxed and also work well for videoing your practice sessions.

If you experience an internet interruption, stay calm, tell the interviewer what is happening on your end of the conversation, and apologize for any delay. While this can be frustrating to the interviewer, if you are proactive and courteous, that will go a long way.

When you ask for the job at the end of the interview, you have the benefit of being able to look at your list, and you can make sure all the important examples are reinforced. You might say, "I hope you can see that my internship, my exchange student experience, and my problem-solving abilities discussed in my marketing project have proven I am well prepared to make a difference in your firm. I can assure you that I can adapt to change because we did not discuss the fact that I had to relocate with my family three times during my high school years. I have learned to assimilate rather quickly because of those moves. I am confident that my leadership training and university education have given me a sound preparation to lead. After talking with you, I feel very strongly that I am a good candidate to make a difference in your firm and I would hope to be able to show you what I can accomplish for you."

Be Upfront with Conflicts

Be forthcoming with any future events you have that will affect your hiring decision. For example, if you are getting married two months after your hiring date, let them know

now that you will need time off. You may need to take it without pay, but at least they will not be shocked and upset when the time off is requested. I accepted a job and knew I had a trip planned, so I told them during the offer conversations. You will find that employers will be very accommodating if they really want you.

Position

Position yourself well enough, and circumstances will do the rest.

—Mason Cooley

Congratulations! You have completed what I know is the best interview you could have given, but the hard work isn't over yet. It is time to review and follow up, which is an integral part of the learning process.

The Final Phase

Review and Follow-Up

Upon completing an interview, you need to write notes to yourself about how you feel the interview went. Make note of positives and negatives. What went well? What could have gone better? What questions surprised you?

Thank You

The second thing you should do right after an interview is send a handwritten "Thank You" note. Recruiters say that a note of appreciation leads interviewers to review candidates in a positive manner more than 80 percent of the time. Always ask for a business card or contact information and, immediately after your interview, write the note and drop it in the first available postal box (remember you already have the envelope addressed and stamped.) The important thing is to send it quickly before the final decision is made. So, before you get in your car, on the train, or go to the airport, mail the card.

If you have experienced a problem with mail speed in the past, it is acceptable to send an email, but it must be specific and thoughtful. Detail your note or email to your interview with regards to content, and you can even use it as one last opportunity to clarify or emphasize your qualifications. According to *CareerBuilder.com*, when asked, hiring managers answered with the following preferences about which forms of gratitude they welcome:

Email	87%
Phone calls	81%

Handwritten notes	38%
Social media	27%
Text message	10%

Unlike handwritten notes, which should be mailed that day, if you choose to use email or a phone call, you should wait several hours or even until the next day to show that it is not just an automatic response. The important thing is to thank your interviewer. You can search for examples of interview "Thank You" messages and pick a format that suits your communication style. In a recent *CareerBuilder* survey, 87 percent of the managers felt that not sending a "Thank You" card or letter showed lack of follow-through from a candidate. It is important!

Referrals and Contacts

The last suggestion for follow-up is to continue to mine for opportunities. A large portion of jobs are filled through referrals, so keep your business cards with you to give to contacts or anyone with whom you would like to stay in touch. One of my recent clients is a golf caddy in the summer, and he exchanges cards at the end of golf rounds. He says something like, "Thank you for allowing me to caddy for you today, here is my card. I would appreciate you asking for me in the future. By the way, can I ask how you spend your time?" Then he might follow with, "Great. I would be interested if you know of any job opportunities. If so, I would like to discuss them with you since I am a business major graduating in a year. Thanks." It makes great sense to be prepared for every opportunity to network.

Finally, be willing to share a job posting if the job is not for you. The "Golden Rule" is to treat others as you would have them treat you; so, if you have an interview, and you know it is not for you, but you know someone who would do well in the job, be willing to refer them. I had a client who referred his friend for a job, and the friend secured the job and has gone on to be a very successful executive in that industry. If you can help someone, do so; they will be willing to help you in return.

Continual Learning

Continue to develop your skills through the books you read and the people you meet, and you will be a changed person.

—Charlie "Tremendous" Jones

Some say that it takes 10,000 hours of practice to become a pro at something. I am not so sure about that. While practice is certainly important, it doesn't take 10,000 hours to learn that a red-colored range coil is hot. You become a pro after that first experience. I think it is more of what you learn from each experience that counts. Likewise, I think it is possible to gain knowledge and professionalism very quickly when you put past experiences to work for your future.

All of your experiences have taught you something, and you have had a lot of experiences. Each one has prepared you to respond differently going forward in life. Sometimes, we just need reminding.

Your Toolbox

As you go through the preparation and interview process, think of it as adding tools to your toolbox; a toolbox that holds a variety of tools that make you different from any other person in history. You are unique, and your experiences are unique, and your tools aid you in pulling this uniqueness together in a cohesive way to create a blueprint of how you are the right person for the right position.

British philosopher James Allen wrote in

his book, *As a Man Thinketh,* that a person is limited only by the thoughts he chooses. This interview process is a guide for you to pull all your experiences into focus so that they shape your thoughts in a manner that supports you.

Kaleidoscope

Life for us is like looking through a kaleidoscope. Think of your experiences like little fragments of color in your scope of life. The more experiences you have, the more colors and pieces you have. There has not been an experience that has not added to your view of life. All these pieces come together to create a beautiful image. In this light, your job in the interview process is to piece together your experiences in a way that presents your image, showing your interviewer just who you are as a person and as a future employee.

Be willing to do the hard work that unsuccessful applicants are not willing to do, and you will find the success you seek. Opportunities abound for those prepared to take the challenge at hand. Be prepared and enjoy the ride!

May God Bless You.

About Phil Hess

Philip Hess' career spans over 60 years as a manager, recruiter, accountant, professor, and preacher. Phil's expertise comes from managing, interviewing, hiring, teaching, or preaching to thousands of individuals and organizations in person or through virtual communication.

He earned a BS in Economics from Juniata College and his MBA from Caldwell University. His career includes 38 years with a Fortune 500 company specializing in general management, operations, merchandising, and college recruiting. Currently he is a public accountant and adjunct professor in accounting, marketing, strategic management, business communications, and ethics.

Phil is considered a turnaround specialist and has led several units to top rankings in the then largest retailer in America.

He continues to expand service to others through his faith as a pulpit supply preacher in the Northeast. He has conducted over 450 services to date.

"Lighting The Way" is Phil's personal and Christian purpose and he strives to expand his caring for others. He formed UP-

WARD CAREER COUNSELING to provide personal interview counseling. It is Phil's prayer this book will help you be successful obtaining the job, career, or education you most surely deserve.

Contact Phil Hess

UpwardCareerCounseling.com

philhessucc@gmail.com

(201) 274 - 6808